# American Furniture

# 1660–1725

## Craig A Gilborn

**COUNTRY LIFE COLLECTORS' GUIDES**

Armchair in the William and Mary style. An instance of wood analysis helping confirm an American origin for a piece that closely follows English models in all other respects. Soft maple and red oak (both American). Probably New England. 1700–1725. The Henry Francis du Pont Winterthur Museum, Delaware.

# Finding Comparisons

Numbers in the margin refer to the page where an illustration may be found

If it could be known, the notion held by most Americans about the England of the colonial period would probably be found to consist of a hodgepodge of courtiers, younger sons, and comely maids, all variously at the mercy of a rich nobleman living amid gilded furniture and leather bindings in an ancestral mansion set in a picturesque landscape. What is the Englishman's mental image of the American colonies? Possibly the following: flinty Puritan patriarchs, tradesmen who mingle piety and profit, and hardy frontiersmen—all so busy wrestling with their souls, business affairs, the Indians or the howling wilderness that they have little energy left over for making a civilisation. Both conceptions contain an element of truth and both reflect the stress that historians have placed upon the differences rather than the similarities between the Old World and the New World.

Conceptions affect our perceptions, which is why the reader is gently cautioned, as he views the illustrations, to avoid committing what an historian of American painting has called the 'frontier fallacy'. Colonial furniture of the period with which we are here concerned, which opens with the Restoration of Charles II and closes shortly before the founding, in 1732, of the colony of Georgia, does not derive its appearance from the deprivations of life on an American frontier. To be sure, there are lapses in the quality of execution, but similar expressions of provinciality can be found in the furniture of the same period throughout Great Britain.

Map of colonial America in 1725. Indicated are the approximate extent of settlement and the principal cities that dominated the economic life of nearby regions.

Our view of colonial American furniture–indeed, of colonial society itself–depends to a large extent upon what we see in English furniture and society of the same period. Our knowledge of English homes of the period is largely based on the work of such outstanding artist-designers as William Kent, whose wealthy patrons, Lord Burlington among them, moved in a cultured and sophisticated world where they were able to commission extravagant buildings incorporating furniture and decoration in the latest fashion. The modest home of a Virginia planter is clearly not comparable with the splendours of Burlington House, but, nevertheless, American furniture and furnishings have undoubtedly suffered by such comparisons being made. Recently published studies of English architecture in which both great and small houses are discussed should help to place American architecture of the colonial period in sharper perspective. Similar studies on furniture are needed before a fair comparison can be made and the **American contribution** properly assessed.

6, 48–53

This writer is inclined to view colonial furniture within a broad Euro-American context that includes some of the following propositions:

1. America was an underdeveloped country during the colonial period, but so was much of Europe, which provided the colonials with centuries of experience in coping with climatic extremes, primitive living conditions, and large tracts of unimproved land.

2. By about 1690, colonial society was beginning to show signs of developing the complex inter-relationships that characterised the mature urbanised societies of Europe. Evidence for this may be seen principally in the seaport cities of Boston, New York, Philadelphia, and several other regional centres of trade.

3. Generally, the larger colonial cities and towns had more direct access to London, by virtue of their location near the ocean, than did many comparable settlements in Europe. The absence of long-lived craft traditions in the colonies might be explained, in part, by a steady exposure of influences coming from London and other centres of taste in Europe.

4. A high percentage of colonial furniture cannot be **identified as**

2 **American** solely on the basis of its overall appearance. In other

words, much colonial furniture closely resembles furniture produced at about the same time in England and the continent.

These and other assumptions which see a close relationship between the cultural materials of the New and the Old Worlds will be touched upon but not examined in any detail in the brief discussion that follows.

Lidded chest with two drawers (Sunflower type). Found near Hartford, Connecticut, these chests constitute one of several types that can be said to be distinctly 'American'. Oak, pine, cherry. 1680–1710. The Henry Francis du Pont Winterthur Museum, Delaware.

# Colonial Homes

Several examples of colonial dwellings and furnished interiors are illustrated to give the reader an idea of the appearance and the direction of development in the colonial arts of the period.

8      The earliest of these is the **Parson Capen House**, built in 1683 at Topsfield, Massachusetts, representing a type that, except for changes in details, appeared throughout New England during the entire colonial period and later. Wood is used unsparingly for almost everything except the brick chimney that forms the core of the house. Furnished interiors of rooms from two other **17th-**

9, 31    **century houses in Massachusetts** are also shown. Period rooms like these are conjectural, based largely upon the accidents of survival, written documents such as household inventories, and curatorial intuition.

Compare these rooms with the description of a Salem interior that remained untouched by fashions after the late 1600s. Writing in 1796, the antiquarian, William Bentley, observed that 'The windows of this house are of the small glass with lead in diamonds & open upon hinges.' Bentley then jotted these fragments in his diary: 'The Doors open with wooded latches. The Chairs are the upright high arm chairs, & the common chairs are the short backed. The tables small & oval, the chest of drawers with knobs, & short swelled legs. The large fire places & the iron for the lamp. The blocks of wood in the corner [Bentley may be referring here to the corner posts which were left exposed in the interiors of most frame houses built before 1725]. The Press for pewter platers with round holes over the door of it. Large stones rolled before the door for steps. Old Dutch maps & map mondes high coloured above a century old. The Beds very low, & the curtains hung upon the walls.'

William Brinton, a farmer and English Quaker, occupied a stone
10   house, **Brinton House**, that was built for him in 1704 in the fertile country about twenty-five miles west of Philadelphia. A mixture of influences may be found in the buildings and furniture
4   of the so-called **Middle Colonies**—New York, New Jersey, Pennsylvania, and Delaware—as might be expected in a region which attracted settlers from every corner of Europe. The **Dutch co-**
32–33   **lonial interior** at the Brooklyn Museum derives its woodwork

The Parson Capen House, built in 1683 for a minister of Topsfield, Massachusetts. Framed and clapboarded houses of the colonial period survive in goodly numbers in New England. Property of the Topsfield Historical Society.

from a house built for the miller, Jan Martense Schenck, about 1675 in Brooklyn, New York. Sash windows like the one in the photograph were introduced to the colonies in the last decade of the century.

The colonial forerunners of the Georgian houses of the 1720s and later did not appear in America until late in the 17th century, or about forty or so years after their prototypes first began appearing in England. **Brafferton Hall**, at Williamsburg, Virginia, followed English and possibly Dutch models for domestic architecture: a symmetrical façade, hipped roof, enriched cornices and doorways, plus other details, some of which were borrowed from the vocabulary of the Renaissance.

Reconstruction of an all-purpose New England 'hall' of about 1710. The house and furniture, as shown here, were made by carpenters, joiners, and turners who often combined several woodworking activities. Slat back armchairs left and right, wainscot chair beyond the fireplace; candlestand far left, lidded chest centre background. The American Museum in Britain, Claverton Manor, Bath, Somerset.

That the years shortly before and after 1700 mark something of a period of transition between the unsophisticated mode of building in the **Parson Capen House** and the formal style of **Brafferton Hall**, is suggested in a comment published in 1705 by Governor Robert Beverley about the plantation houses of Virginia: 'Of late they have made their Stories much higher than formerly, and their Windows large, and sasht with Cristal Glass.' Beverley, a stern critic of the undue reliance of Virginia's planters upon English manufactures, mentioned that 'they adorn their Apartments with rich furniture,' and, elsewhere, that Virginians 'always contrive to have large Rooms, that they may be cool in

8

11

The Brinton House, Delaware County, Pennsylvania. Built in 1704, this stone house combines traditional and fashionable elements. Similar influences may be seen in the furniture of the period. Property of the Chester County Historical Society.

Brafferton Hall, built in 1723 in Williamsburg, Virginia, as a school for Indian children with funds from the estate of Robert Boyle, the English physician.

The 'Flock Room' at the Winterthur Museum, deriving its name from the English wall covering. The panelling, painted grey-blue with marbleised details, comes from a house built about 1715 in Morattico, Virginia. The Henry Francis du Pont Winterthur Museum, Delaware.

Summer'. The **Flock Room** at the Winterthur Museum consists of grey-blue panelling and overmantel paintings from Virginia, an English flock wall covering, and furniture from New England and the Middle Colonies.

Life is more cluttered and vastly more interesting than the antiques that stand in their appointed places in our museums. An observation from the past can suddenly illuminate these mute objects by giving us an idea of the life that flowed on around them. The following verses are from *The Sotweed Factor*, a satirical poem written about 1708 by Ebenezer Cook, who had his worldly narrator take careful note of the rustic manners and home of a Maryland planter.

> For Planters Tables, you must know
> Are free for all that come and go,
> While Pone, with Milk and Mush well stor'd,
> In wooden Dishes grac'd the Board,
> With Hominy and Sider-Sap,
> Which scarce an *English* Dog would lap,
> Well stuff'd with Fat and Bacon fry'd,
> And with Melasses dulcify'd.
> Than out our Landlord pulls his Pouch,
> As greasy as the Leather Couch
> On which he sat, and streight begun
> To load with Weed his Indian Gun,
> In Length scarce longer than one's Finger,
> Or that for which the Ladies linger.
> His pipe smoak'd out, with awful Grace,
> With Aspect grave and solemn Pace,
> The Reverend Sir, walks to a Chest,
> Of all his Furniture the best,
> Closely confin'd within a Room,
> Which seldom felt the Weight of Broom.

Satire permitted exaggeration; but there is more truth than not in Cook's caricature. A similar scene, not subject to ridicule, was witnessed by this writer when he was the guest in the home of a family whose leadership in Virginia's politics dates back to the period covered by this book.

# The
# Furniture

Extant furniture of the middle colonial period, i.e., 1660–1725, reflects most of the impulses, stylistic and technological, found among the colonials' European counterparts, especially in England, at about the same time. Tradition and innovation, two forces responsible for much of the diversity and creative vigour of the 17th century, are clearly evident in the furniture of the period, and it is under these two broad and admittedly simplistic headings that we will view the three or four basic functional forms—seats, tables, case pieces, and sleeping furniture.

What constitutes tradition or innovation? If a newly made piece resembled what one's grandparents had in their homes, then it was traditional. Distinctions between old fashioned and 'new fangled' were pretty clear to everyone, their personal or factional preferences for one or the other notwithstanding. Inventories of furnishings, drawn up by two men appointed by the court at the time of a householder's death, frequently used terms such as 'old' and 'new fashion' in identifying pieces of furniture in colonial homes. Innovations in furniture can be seen partly as the result of a desire for comfort, convenience and grace, qualities not to be found, with a very few exceptions, in the furniture of James I's time or earlier.

## Seats

16, 17    The **all-turned stick chairs**, resembling those armchairs used by the nobility and churchmen at least as early as the 10th century, were perhaps the oldest *type* of seats used in colonial

America. Names of colonial personages are often associated with these turned armchairs, as well as **joined examples**, indicating that the 'great' chair in 17th-century America retained much of its older role as a seat of authority and distinction. Chairs with **double and single ranks of spindles** are identified in America as 'Brewster' and 'Carver' chairs, presumably after William Brewster and John Carver, two Pilgrim leaders who are believed to have owned similar chairs. Interestingly, armchairs are occasionally referred to in English documents as 'carvers'.

Colonial household inventories refer to 'great' chairs, meaning, we believe, armchairs like the turned examples just mentioned, as well as **'joined'** or **'wainscot'** (terms also used) chairs. The

Turned 'great' chair, the double ranks of spindles denoting it as the Brewster type. These 'stick' chairs had changed little since the 10th century. Hickory and ash. Massachusetts. About 1650. The Metropolitan Museum of Art, New York, Gift of Mrs J. Insley Blair, 1951.

9, 18, 47

16, 17

9, 18, 47

'great' chair at The Essex Institute, Salem, has considerably more
18   **carved decoration** than most colonial wainscot chairs; the
carved figures or grotesques applied to the stiles (outer uprights)
of the back are perhaps the earliest examples of 'sculpture' sur-
viving from the early colonial period. A simpler—and perhaps
9    more typical—**wainscot chair** is on display in the American
Museum in Britain, at Claverton Manor, Bath.

A versatile contrivance, perhaps more interesting than it was
19   useful, was the **chair-table**. A Pilgrim inventory of mid century
mentions 'a little chaire table with a small carpet'. These pieces,
usually with circular tops and incorporating a drawer under
the seat, were made into the 19th century.

Turned armchair. The construction
was the turner's attempt to impart
comfort by raking the back slightly.
This chair descended in the Stryker
family, of New York. 17th century.
The Metropolitan Museum of Art,
New York, Rogers Fund, 1941.

Joined 'great' chair (wainscot armchair). The carved decoration, as elaborate as can be found on these chairs, mixes medieval, Renaissance and Baroque motifs. Attributed to Thomas Dennis (about 1638–1706) or an apprentice. Red (American) and white oak. Essex County, Massachusetts. The Essex Institute, Salem, Massachusetts.

9, 21     **Slat back chairs** were a variation of the all-turned chair. Two specimens having the more ample turnings that are associated with the turnery of the 17th century may be seen at the American

21     Museum in Britain. A **slat back armchair** at Winterthur has the higher back and the ball-and-disc turnings that characterise some of these chairs after about 1700. That tall slatted chairs date at least from the first years of the century is indicated by an **oil**

20     **sketch of about 1705** in which Johannes Kelpius is shown seated at a table in one of these chairs. All sorts of turned chairs were produced in America from this early period down to the present century, and assigning the usual two to three decade period of

Chair-table, a hybrid combining the functions of a chair, table and chest (a drawer under the seat). White oak and pine. New England. 1675–1700. Length of top 53 in. The Metropolitan Museum of Art, New York, Gift of Mrs Russell Sage, 1909.

Oil sketch of the mystic, Johannes Kelpius (died 1708), seated in a slat back armchair of the type shown in the next illustration. Oil on canvas. Philadelphia. About 1705. Height 9 in. The Historical Society of Pennsylvania, Philadelphia.

Slat back armchair, a type popular from the 1690s into the 19th century. Maple, hickory, with rush seat. Possibly Pennsylvania. 1700–1740 or later. The Henry Francis du Pont Winterthur Museum, Delaware.

manufacture must be qualified in view of the continued popularity of these chairs and of the turner's or chairmaker's ability to 'turn out' most of the shapes made by his predecessors.

More kinds of craftsmen were engaged in manufacturing chairs and other seats than any other form of furniture: joiners, turners, carpenters, cabinetmakers, chairmakers, cane chairmakers, upholsterers, and possibly carvers were capable of producing part or all of certain kinds of seats. The proliferation of crafts began occurring at about the time of the Restoration in 1660, so that the older idea of the maker of chairs as principally a joiner or turner rapidly became less tenable. For example, English upholsterers sold upholstered seats like the chair illustrated with a **turkey-work back and seat** to buyers in England and the colonies.

22

Two fashionable side chairs. *left* American walnut, white oak. Tradition holds that it was made in 1699 in Crosswicks, New Jersey. *right* Cromwellian type. Maple, covered with English turkeywork. New England. 1650–1715. The Henry Francis du Pont Winterthur Museum, Delaware.

The chair just cited, called a Cromwellian chair, and its companion with **spiral turnings**, belong to the earliest type of sitting furniture of cabinetwork quality to be found in the colonies. Both follow essentially the same construction and form—turnings joined by mortice and tenon joints and having square backs. They constitute a striking departure from the traditional chairs we have seen thus far. Chairs with turkeywork were popular in the colonies: a 1691 inventory has '6 Turkey work chairs' in the best room of a Roxbury home, and by 1749 another inventory in the same Massachusetts town has relegated 'In the Back Chamber . . . 6 old Turk:work Chairs'.

When Americans speak of William and Mary chairs they generally mean the high backed seats of leather or cane which

Banister back armchair, combining elements found in high style English chairs of 1685–1715. Maple with splint seat. Attributed to John Gaines II (about 1697–1748), of Ipswich, Massachusetts. About 1715–1740. The Henry Francis du Pont Winterthur Museum, Delaware.

were introduced to England with the Dutch court of William III and its French-born designer, Daniel Marot. The **leather example** shown is as elaborate as can be found from the period; the leaf and C-scroll carvings on the back and between the front legs provide the richest and most characteristic touch of the William and Mary style in America. Some caned furniture was later covered with leather: a document of 1726 in Pennsylvania notes 'making leather seats to cane Chairs'.

Colonial craftsmen were seldom innovators, but some of them took elements from fashionable European furniture and combined them in pieces that are fresh and harmoniously integrated. The **banister back chair** seen here and **others like it** are associated with a family of turners and chairmakers who worked at Portsmouth, New Hampshire, and also at Ipswich, Massachusetts. It is attributed to John Gaines II (1697–1748), the son of a turner and himself the father and grandfather of a chairmaker and cabinetmaker. John Gaines II was manufacturing chairs like this long after the William and Mary style had lost favour in London. The writer views this chair as one of the few examples of **furniture in an American idiom**—not great or unique, but a noteworthy contribution nonetheless.

Easy chairs were not generally adopted among fashionable colonials until the second quarter of the 18th century. This is supported by inventories and by the few survivors which **incorporate elements of the William and Mary style**. Products of upholsterers working with turners or joiners, easy chairs date from the reign of James I, but they did not achieve wide popularity in England until about 1700. The crest and vertical proportions of the **colonial wing chair** illustrated occur in the chairs which are in the **Flock Room** at Winterthur. Also of interest are the shaped skirt, which happily complements the back, the double roll of the arm, interpreted as an indication of a New England origin, and the small 'Spanish' feet, which appear elsewhere in this book in a variety of forms.

The **settee with turkeywork upholstery** at The Essex Institute is essentially a wider version, with arms, of the **Cromwellian chair** that we saw previously. This settee is illustrated

2

23, 29

6, 48–53

25

25
12–13

25

22

Easy chair in a European red silk velvet (not original). The vertical proportions, crest, shaped skirt and 'Spanish' feet are stylistic elements of the William and Mary Period. Maple and oak. New England. 1710–1725. Height 51 in. The Henry Francis du Pont Winterthur Museum, Delaware.

Settee with turkeywork upholstery. A problem piece, probably owned by a colonial, but with several conflicting traditions that it is American, English or French Huguenot in origin. Maple. 1680–1715. The Essex Institute, Salem, Massachusetts.

partly because it is representative of the problems that the student of American furniture often encounters in his work. Several traditions hold that the settee is American, English, and French. A similar settee was purchased at auction in 1819 by the Reverend Bentley, who called it a 'settle' and reported that Dr Holyoke, ninety-one years old, recalled seeing the piece eighty years earlier in the home of the Appleton family. The settee illustrated was given to the Essex Historical Society (now The Essex Institute), in Salem, perhaps as early as the 1820s, but whether it is the same settee acquired by Bentley, a resident of Salem, is not determined. A point worth making here is that large quantities of furniture were shipped to the colonies from

Settee or settle which attempts to unite the protective form of the medieval settle with fashionable touches borrowed from the Restoration settee. Walnut and leather. Pennsylvania. 1700–1740. The Metropolitan Museum of Art, New York. Gift in memory of Mrs J. Amory Haskell by her children, 1945.

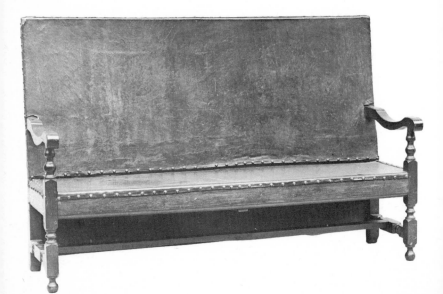

England during the colonial period; except for a few pieces
32–33 handed down in families of Dutch extraction (e.g., the **kas**, a type of large wardrobe from Holland), very little has been done to trace European furniture having a long history of ownership in America.

Still undecided whether to be functional or fashionable is the
26 **walnut and leather settle** (or is it a settee?) shown here. The protective function of the medieval settle is retained in the high back and its extension almost to the floor. The shaped arms and turned supports are modest gestures of a sort that might have appealed to a Quaker or some of the other plain-living people of Pennsylvania who sought an aesthetic at once suitable to their

Settle with hood, fielded panels, black paint. White pine. New England.
1710–1750. Height 62¼ in, width 73 in. The Henry Francis du Pont Winterthur Museum, Delaware.

religious beliefs and worthy of their improved station in colonial society. This example was probably made by a furniture specialist, perhaps a cabinetmaker, whereas the **white pine settle with a hood**, with its use of large boards and fielded panels (raised panels with a wide, flat surface surrounded by mouldings), suggests that it might have been built by a carpenter-joiner trained principally in finishing house interiors, especially in the construction of panelling. Furniture with fielded panels occurred in all the colonies – this settle is believed to be from New England – but the largest quantity is to be found in Pennsylvania. Welsh furniture of the 18th century reflects a fondness for the fielded panel, and it is entirely possible that this predilection arrived in William Penn's haven with craftsmen who came from Wales.

27

The colonists were no exception to the universal search for something to sit on. We have seen a few select examples of seats that survived. No one, however, preserved the 'block or two in the corner instead of chairs' that Madame Sarah Kemble Knight noticed in the 'little Hutt' where she briefly stayed during her solitary journey on horseback from Boston to New York in 1704.

**Sleeping furniture**

Our predecessors demonstrated a remarkable ability to sleep almost anywhere. What we have come to expect as a seven or eight hour sleep was, for the majority of colonials, more like a succession of naps. Madame Knight's salty comments about her accommodation at an inn in Rye, New York, confirms what other commentators, before and after, have told us about the tribulations of the traveller:

'. . . arriving at my apartment [I] found it to be a little Leanto Chamber furnisht amongst other Rubbish with a High Bedd and a Low one, a Long Table, a Bench and a Bottomless chair. Little Miss went to scratch up my Kennell w$^{ch}$ Russelled as if shee'd bin in the Barn amongst the Husks. . . nevertheless being exceeding weary, down I laid my poor Carkes [carcass] (never more tired) and found my Covering as scanty as my Bed was hard. Annon I heard another Russelling noise in Ye Room – called to know the matter – Little miss said shee was making a Bed for the men . . .'

Madame Knight spent the remainder of the night 'Setting up by the Fire till Light'.

A year later, in 1705, Governor Robert Beverley called attention to the hospitality among Southern planters: 'And the poor Planters, who have but one Bed, will often sit up, or lie upon a Form or Couch all Night, to make room for a weary Traveler. . .' Several of the seats that we saw in the preceding section could have been pressed into service for sleeping; the **leather settee** and the **settle with a hood** are two candidates, as was the **colonial easy chair**, which could serve as a refuge from a bed infested with bedbugs. The 'couch' mentioned by Beverley was probably a **daybed** such as those that also appear in these pages.

26
27
25

12–13, 29

The 'Williams Room' with painted woodwork from a house of about 1710 from Lebanon, Connecticut. A combination of William and Mary and Queen Anne elements can be seen in the desk and bookcase, the side chairs, and the daybed. The Henry Francis du Pont Winterthur Museum, Delaware.

We think of 'bed' as a combination of frame, mattress and bedclothes, but to the colonials the term meant the soft furnishings which might just as well be thrown on the floor as placed on the rope webbing of the bedstead. The **trundle bed**, here covered with a heavy green wool rug, consists of these elements, and it might be the type of 'low' bed mentioned by the unfortunate Madame Knight.

The bedstead was not, at this time, generally regarded as an isolated piece of furniture. Few, if any, stylish colonial bedsteads can be dated with confidence before about 1740. The paucity of bedsteads, together with the fact that bed coverings and hangings consistently received a much larger valuation in inventories than did the frames on which they were hung, indicates that the posts,

Trundle bed covered with a wool rug. There are no American bedsteads that can be dated before 1740, but this undoubtedly resembles earlier styles. White pine and ash (American). New England. 18th century. Length 61 in. The Henry Francis du Pont Winterthur Museum, Delaware.

*right* Bedchamber installed in the hall of the Abraham Browne House near Waltham, Massachusetts. The bed curtains and fringed valance, of blue and green wools embroidered on cotton twill (crewel), carry the initials 'A.P.' and '1674', and are English or possibly American. The Society for the Preservation of New England Antiquities, Boston, Massachusetts.

tester and other portions of the bed were meant to be concealed behind the abundant folds of the valance and curtains. This

31   point is clearly indicated by the **matching set of hangings** displayed on the bed in the Abraham Browne House, in Massachusetts. One of the curtains carries the crewelwork date 1674 and the initials A.P. A simpler, somewhat primitive method of enclosing the bed is implied in the statement, quoted above, by the Reverend William Bentley, who noted 'The Beds very low, & the curtains hung upon the walls'.

    Colonial documents occasionally refer to panelled or box beds, such as were found in northern Europe, including parts of Britain. None seems to have survived in American historic houses, but

32–33   **two enclosed beds**, modelled after examples in Holland, have

Room from the Brooklyn house of Jan Martense Schenck, built about 1675 and installed with American and European furnishings of the period. Large Dutch wardrobe or *kas* on right; enclosed bed behind curtains; dressing table under mirror. The Brooklyn Museum, New York.

been installed in a Dutch colonial room from New York, at the Brooklyn Museum.

## Tables

Tables, by themselves, convey an air of incompletion which is not to be found among seats, beds, and case furniture. The table has taken its cues from other things, among them the requirements of the sitter, who must normally be able to place his legs under the table. Hence tables look best when seen **in company with other things** that ordinarily belong with them—with chairs, stools, flanked by forms or benches, or covered with a turkey carpet and a few household furnishings.

12–13, 31

The comparative anonymity of the table is also illustrated by the apparent indifference of any one group of craftsmen in capturing a major part of table manufacture; there were no 'table makers' as such, though men advertised themselves as chairmakers, cabinetmakers, upholsterers, and the like. Tables do not appear among the nine headings of furniture being shipped from England to the colonies, a fact that puzzled R.W. Symonds, the noted English furniture historian, who thought it 'more likely that tables were not exported' than that they were included among the two headings 'Joinery Ware' and 'Turnery Ware'. Tables were shipped, however, as letters indicate; William Byrd instructed his London agents, in 1689, to send him '1 small, 1 middling, and 1 large ovall table'.

35

The **trestle table** at the Metropolitan Museum of Art would seem to exemplify the rougher, less accomplished work that carpenters turned out. Accustomed to building houses and similar wood structures, their attempts at decoration were limited to simple effects such as **chamfering** the sharp corners of exposed beams in house interiors. Each of the three trestles of this table has had its corners cut in similar fashion, as have those of the table displayed in **the 17th-century room** at the American Museum in Britain. These demountable tables, along with **turned great chairs**, are direct descendants of the spacious, communal hall of the Middle Ages.

9, 31

9

16

35

The American **joined table and two forms** or benches show the heavy framed work, usually oak, that was produced principally by joiners. Colonial inventories make reference to 'long,' 'great,' 'framed,' and 'joined' tables, but the application of these terms to existing tables remains conjectural. The table at the Philadelphia Museum of Art has a removable top. Other colonial oblong tables have fixed tops or they can be enlarged by means of a folding leaf that rests on a swinging gate or by a leaf that

Trestle table. Of ancient lineage, these tables were easily stored and quickly assembled. Few survive from our period. Oak and pine. New England. 17th century. Length 146½ in. The Metropolitan Museum of Art, New York, Gift of Mrs Russell Sage, 1909.

Framed table and a pair of joint forms. The top of the table is removable and consists of two planks joined by a cleat. Table: oak, possibly Pennsylvania, 1690–1715. Forms: pear wood, Pennsylvania. The Philadelphia Museum of Art, Pennsylvania.

drops into place when the frame of the table is drawn apart. An inventory of 1678 alludes to 'one frame Table with a pine Leafe'.

36, 37, 38 **Several decorative styles** may be detected in these tables, most particularly as revealed in the turnings of their legs. The 36 **gate-leg table** at the Metropolitan Museum of Art, having a trapezoidal frame and a folding, marbleised top, has the eccentric form, bulbous legs, and applied spindle-and-boss decoration of furniture influenced by the Mannerist style of the late 16th 47 and early 17th centuries. The **court cupboard** at the Winterthur Museum reflects similar influences. Such pieces were made in

Gate-leg table with folding top. The top is marbleised. Oak and maple. Essex County, Massachusetts. 1675–1700. Diameter of top 36 in. The Metropolitan Museum of Art, New York, Gift of Mrs J. Insley Blair, 1951.

the colonies until about 1700, and they may be seen to have been the joiner's last 'conceit' in the manufacture of furniture which directly reflected the programmatic or stylish trends that had taken place earlier in Europe.

37    Spiral turnings like those of the **drop-leaf table** at the Winterthur Museum date from the Restoration to about the turn of the century, though there were precedents for the spiral motif before 1660 in European designs for furniture. Such turnings,

12–13 seen also in a chair and in several objects in the **Flock Room** at Winterthur, are echoes of the Baroque style in the New World.

Drop-leaf table with spiral-turned legs. American walnut and white pine. Middle Colonies. 1680–1720. Top (maximum) $55\frac{1}{4}$ in. The Henry Francis du Pont Winterthur Museum, Delaware.

Another motif of the Baroque style is the **vase form**, illustrated here in the vase and cup turnings of the large mahogany table that originally belonged to George III's Superintendent for Indian Affairs. The vase turning may be observed in some of the furniture of the early 17th century, but the allusion to the vase became clearer in the late 1600s as turners reduced the bandings and other turnings to achieve the lighter, crisper, and more delicate effects, made possible, in part, by the use of hard woods like walnut, maple, and cherry.

The leaf table with an oval top, compact and easy to move, was much more suited than its long counterpart to the smaller, more intimate domestic settings of the late 17th century and afterwards. William Penn, in 1685, asked his American steward to have made

*left* Gate-leg table, confiscated during the Revolution from the home of Sir William Johnson (1715–1774), Superintendent of Indian Affairs for George III. Mahogany, tulip, red gum. New York. 1700–1750. Oval top $78\frac{1}{2}$ in. The Albany Institute of History and Art, New York.

*right* Tea-table. An early and important example, originally owned by Peter Schuyler (died 1724), first mayor of Albany. Cherry with white pine. New York. 1700–1724. The Henry Francis du Pont Winterthur Museum, Delaware.

'two or three eating tables for twelve, eight and five persons with falling leaves in them,' and the Boston diarist, Samuel Sewall, reported in 1719 that guests in his home 'Had a very good Diner, at four tables, two in the best Room.' The leaves of the **drop-leaf**
37 **table** at Winterthur are supported by wooden bars that slide out from the frame. A more typical means of support was the gate leg which swung underneath the leaf, one version being
36 illustrated by the **gate-leg table with folding top** at the Metro-
32–33, 38 politan Museum and another by **drop-leaf tables** having one and two gate legs supporting each of two semicircular leaves.

Prosperity, improvements in technology, and extended communications by means of trade, travel and printed materials created a jumping-off point for the unprecedented flowering of

Dressing table with inlaid top (see next illustration). A form of unclear purpose, these tables go by various names, depending upon detail and whim. Walnut with birch inlay. Pennsylvania. Probably 1724. Height 30 in. The Philadelphia Museum of Art, Pennsylvania.

Inlaid top of dressing table. Incription, ANNO, 1724, FIAT, E M. The Philadelphia Museum of Art, Pennsylvania.

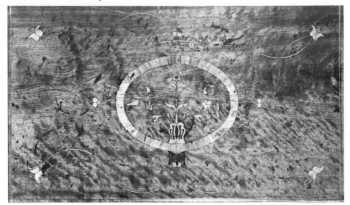

the domestic arts during the 18th century. Americans, colonial artisans and their ambitious patrons, reaped the benefits of these economic developments no less than their counterparts abroad, though the colonial response was derivative and considerably less extravagant than the productions for England's wealthiest families.

The furniture of about 1690 to 1710 seems to have anticipated these subsequent events. Variations of traditional furniture forms were invented and stimulated new variants as patrons, designers, and artisans sought accessories that would be appropriate to novel ritualised behaviour such as tea drinking, dressing, and dining. The proliferation of types of furniture is suggested by 39, 40, 42 the **tea-table**, the **dressing table** and the **serving table** (the **tea-** 39 **table** originally owned by Peter Schuyler is one of the few colonial examples in the William and Mary style). Spurring these efforts were specialists and the cabinetmaker, the latter first specialising in the construction and veneering of case furniture but later appropriating the work of other crafts so that buyers increasingly looked to him for furniture 'in the latest taste' for their homes.

The appearance of cabinetwork (and it was not the simple matter that may seem implied here) corresponded with the arrival of the William and Mary style in the colonies in the late 17th century. The tables mentioned above combine many of the features of this style, which, like all of the fashionable furniture of the century, was really a composite of decorative motifs borrowed from the furniture of all the nations of western Europe, particularly France, the Netherlands, and Flanders. Characteristics are tapered legs, cross stretchers, and ball or Spanish feet. 40, 51 **Inlays and veneers** are found almost for the first time in American furniture, and these, together with brass tear-drop pulls, pendants, and, most importantly, a conscious effort to use proportion and manipulate solids and voids by such means as **shap-** 40, 58 **ing the skirt**, are among the other elements that were introduced with the William and Mary style and the early work of the cabinetmaker in America.

The widespread distribution of similar forms is indicated by a

40, 42, 43 number of **low drawered tables** which are thought to have been made in Pennsylvania, New England, and New York. Recent usage calls these 'lowboys', perhaps because they sometimes 57, 58 accompany larger chests known as '**highboys**'. Their purpose is unclear, though most probably they were meant to be used as 32–33 dressing tables. A dressing or **side table with large scroll legs** is displayed under the mirror in the Dutch colonial room at the 42 Brooklyn Museum. The octagonal top of the **serving table** at the Metropolitan Museum of Art, with its marquetry decoration and an inset slate panel, is believed to have been imported from Switzerland and placed on a frame made in New England. Only a small number of these serving tables survive.

Serving table with top of slate and marquetry. The tops of these are believed to have been imported from Switzerland. Frame and legs: cherry, birch, pine, maple. New England. 1700–1725. The Metropolitan Museum of Art, New York, Gift of George Coe Graves, 1930.

12–13
Small 'occasional' tables abounded, some of which served

9
equally well as either a table or as a stool. A small **candlestand** is on view at the American Museum in Britain, and a **table with**

29
**an oval top**, triangular frame, and raked legs is shown next to the daybed in a room from Connecticut at the Winterthur Museum.

## Case furniture

Case furniture, used for storage and the last of the four basic furniture forms to be discussed, had its origins in the ancient coffer and chest. It afforded the colonial woodworker greater opportunity to display his inventiveness through **ornamenta-**
44, 46, 48
**tion by carving, turning, painting**, the application of **split**

Dressing table or lowboy, apparently the companion to the Clement high chest (see 58). Height 29¾ in. The Henry Francis du Pont Winterthur Museum, Delaware.

**spindles**, **mouldings**, and other elements, or a combination of all of these, as shown in the Winterthur Museum's '**Vocabulary**
**Chest**' from Massachusetts.

**Lidded chests without drawers** or **with one or two drawers** declined in popularity (except possibly among German settlers) late in the first quarter of the 18th century, by which time they

Lidded chest. The carved motifs and three-panel form are common in extant colonial chests of the 1600s. This has a Maryland history. White oak. The Baltimore Museum of Art, Maryland, Gift of Mr & Mrs Arnold Hampson. *opposite* Detail of carved ornamentation.

49, 50 were being supplanted by **chests of drawers**. Simple six-board chests were made, but most survivors are framed and of the type 44 that joiners produced. The **white oak chest** at the Baltimore Museum, believed to have a Maryland origin, employs both the form and carved decoration found in English furniture of the 16th and early 17th centuries.

**Court cupboards** like those illustrated exist in comparatively large numbers, substantiating what they already impress upon our senses – that they were the most valued pieces of furniture in the Anglo-American home of the 1600s. Almost all are from New England, an important exception being the court cupboard with a Virginia history at the Museum of Early Southern Decorative Arts, Winston-Salem, North Carolina, which has a **secondary**

**wood of yellow pine**, a feature generally confined to furniture from the South. Very little Southern furniture survives from this

Court cupboard, mentioned in a Virginia Will of about 1700 as an 'old court cupboard'. Important and rare, the yellow pine interior confirms a Southern history. Oak, yellow pine. Before 1675. Height 49 in. The Museum of Early Southern Decorative Arts, Winston-Salem, North Carolina.

period. The open stages of this cupboard are closer to the medieval idea of the cupboard as a raised platform ('cup board') on which valued objects were displayed and dispensed at meals.

47    The **court cupboard from Massachusetts** represents a later development, being unsuited to service as a buffet, though retaining open surfaces for display and an enclosed section for securing silver and other costly items under lock and key. The dilution of these earlier forms that has occurred in the poly-

48    chromed **press cupboard** at the Henry Ford Museum, Dearborn,

Court cupboard and a joined 'great' chair, both oak and possibly made in Essex County, Massachusetts. The drawer front has the incised date 1684. The Henry Francis du Pont Winterthur Museum, Delaware.

*left* Press cupboard with polychrome
decoration and the name
HANNAH BARNARD. Oak, pine, maple.
Connecticut River Valley, near Hadley,
Massachusetts. 1695–1715. The Henry Ford
Museum, Dearborn, Michigan.

*right* Chest of drawers. The painted
decoration and mouldings are probably by
the same hand that made the press cupboard.
Red and white oak, chestnut, hard pine.
The Henry Francis du Pont Winterthur
Museum, Delaware.

Michigan, suggests that the maker was trying to adapt a respected but outmoded form to the tastes of a younger generation.

Compartmentalising surfaces, a practice for which the 17th-century joiner showed a special fondness, is indicated in the painted panels of the cupboard just mentioned and a **chest of** 49 **drawers** that is apparently by the same hand. These pieces, dating from the early 18th century, seem to be referring back to the compartments which had been achieved earlier by applied mouldings; the second and third tiers of drawers of the **chest** 50 **attributed to Thomas Dennis** are single drawers. The **manner** 51 **of applying mouldings** to the drawer front is shown in a detail.

Chest of drawers incorporating the decorative techniques of carving, painting, applied mouldings and split spindles. Red and white oak, sycamore. Attributed to Thomas Dennis, Ipswich. Inscribed 1678. Height 42 in. The Henry Francis du Pont Winterthus Museum, Delaware.

An American 'idiom' was achieved in several **groups of case** **pieces** made in New England, particularly in the Connecticut River Valley, during the last thirty years or so of our period. Precedents for the forms and individual decorative motifs of these can be found in European furniture of the 17th century and earlier, but the integration and treatment of their ornamentation has no counterpart, so far as the writer knows, anywhere else.

A large number of **lidded chests with a tulip and leaf design** in shallow relief can be traced to the area near the border that separates Massachusetts and Connecticut. Identified as the 'Hadley type' of chest, after a town in Massachusetts, these are sometimes found with traces of red, black, and polychromed paint. A short distance to the south, in the area of Hartford, Connecticut,

Detail of drawer, showing grooved side nailed into rebated front. The Henry Francis du Pont Winterthur Museum, Delaware.

are the **'Sunflower' chests**, so called because of the distinctive carved rosettes (possibly a Tudor rose) that appear on the middle panel between matching panels having a tulip design. Still further south, near the mouth of the Connecticut River, are a variety of case pieces, somewhat later in date, which have an overall painted decoration of flowers, vines, and an occasional bird applied to a case which has the slab construction of early cabinetwork rather than the frame and panels of traditional joinery. One of the **'Saybrook' chests,** dated 1724, combines a

*left* Lidded chest with drawer (Hadley type). About 115 chests with variants of this chip-carved design are known, many traceable to the area near the Massachusetts and Connecticut border in the Connecticut River Valley. White oak, pine, beech. 1680–1710. The Henry Francis du Pont Winterthur Museum, Delaware.

*right* Lidded chest with two drawers (Saybrook type). Similar pieces come from an area near the mouth of the Connecticut River. Tulip, white pine. Possibly Charles Guillam (d. 1727). Painted inscription: In Ye 1724, S H. Height $47\frac{1}{4}$ in. The Henry Francis du Pont Winterthur Museum, Delaware.

lidded chest, two drawers, and a compartment hidden beneath the bottom drawer.

Dutch influence in the colonies was felt directly through second and third generation families of Dutch extraction who, in many instances, maintained close ties with relatives and business associates in Holland long after 1664 when New Netherlands fell under English rule and was renamed New York. Equally strong but more subtly expressed were indirect influences which brought continental designs and craft techniques to the colonies

by way of Dutch and Flemish craftsmen and artists working in England. Direct evidence of the Dutch presence is provided by the *kasten* or large wardrobes that are found almost exclusively in the Hudson River Valley and in nearby areas settled by the Dutch. A comparison of a **colonial kas** with a **Dutch-made example** having a long history of ownership in New York illustrates the reduction of a European form to the most basic of terms.

54

32–33

55       **Grisaille decoration** of pendant fruit, ribbons, and flowers

may be found on the front and sides of several *kasten* from New York. Like most wardrobes (the German *Schrank* appeared later), these generally were constructed in several sections for easier moving. China was displayed on the *kas*; a Dutch colonial inventory of 1692 mentions a 'Holland cubbart furnished with earthenware and porcelain'.

The colonial high chest, popularly known today as a highboy (the term 'tallboy' was used as early as 1769 in England), had its counterparts in England at the same time; but so many were made in all of the thirteen colonies, that we are inclined to believe there was greater enthusiasm for them in America than in England.

57 **Japanned high chests**, decorated with gilded chinoiserie figures on a black ground, in imitation of Chinese lacquerwork, are found in New England during the first half of the 18th century. Japanners were advertising their services in Boston in 1712 and later.

58 A **high chest signed by the maker** and dated 1726 documents the persistence of the William and Mary style in the colonies well after the time the style had ceased to be fashionable in London. Samuel Clement is also believed to have made the **companion**
43 **dressing table**; similarities shared by the two pieces include the shaping and moulding of the skirt, the double half-round mouldings around the drawer openings, the inlay decoration on the drawer fronts, and the use of red gum with ash and elm. However, the legs differ in small details and the dovetails were allowed to show in the dressing table whereas they were concealed in the high chest. According to the author of a book on inventories of rural households in colonial New England, high chests and dressing tables were seldom listed in rooms at ground level and were found, instead, in the upstairs chambers.

59 The **walnut writing cabinet** at Colonial Williamsburg is of considerable interest because it carries the stamped name and date 'Edward Evans 1707', thereby demonstrating that cabinetmakers and patrons in the colonies were in touch with design ideas that were still fairly new in England. A single half-round moulding surrounds the opening for the drawers. This feature is
57, 58, regarded as an indication of manufacture prior to **pieces having**
60, 61 **the double mouldings**, a rough rule of thumb that seems to

Japanned high chest (highboy). 'Japanning' was practised in England and the colonies in imitation of Chinese lacquerwork. Maple and pine. New England. 1700–1725. Height $62\frac{1}{2}$ in. The Metropolitan Museum of Art, New York, Purchase, 1940, Joseph Pulitzer Bequest.

High chest (highboy), signed by Samuel Clement and dated 1726. The bolection moulding pulls out to reveal a shallow drawer. Red gum, ash, elm. Flushing, Long Island. Height 72 in. The Henry Francis du Pont Winterthur Museum, Delaware.

Inscription in lower centre drawer: This was made in ye Year 1726/ By me Samuel Clement of Flushing/ June ye.

Writing cabinet on chest of drawers, perhaps the earliest example of signed and dated American furniture. Walnut with cedar and pine. Philadelphia. Height 66$\frac{1}{2}$ in. Colonial Williamsburg, Virginia.

Detail of branded inscription: Edward Evans 1707.

*left* Desk and bookcase, a rare colonial version of an Anglo-Dutch form of the William and Mary period. Walnut and poplar. Philadelphia. 1700–1735. Height 90 in. The Philadelphia Museum of Art, Pennsylvania.

*right* Slope-front desk, a specimen of the cabinetmaker's ability to veneer, which helped revolutionise the furniture-making crafts. Walnut veneers, maple and oak inlays, secondary woods of chestnut, maple, white pine. Massachusetts. 1700–1725. The Henry Francis du Pont Winterthur Museum, Delaware.

58　work when applied to Samuel Clement's **high chest** with these latter mouldings and the inscribed date 1726.

Veneers were frequently omitted from case furniture which usually would be veneered in Europe. The cabinet just discussed
60　is an example, as is the **desk and bookcase** in the Philadelphia Museum. However, veneered colonial furniture is by no means
61　rare for this period. The **slope-front desk** from Massachusetts, one of a number of desks similarly treated, has a burl walnut veneer with maple and oak inlays in a herringbone pattern. The widespread adoption of mahogany in the 1730s and 1740s temporarily dampened the interest in veneered furniture in

Looking-glass. Walnut veneer and pine base. Frame probably American. 1700–1725. Height about 46 in. The Henry Francis du Pont Winterthur Museum, Delaware.

England and America for a period of about fifteen to thirty years.

60    The **desk and bookcase** appeared in various stylistic guises throughout the 18th century and into the next century, but it always retained the essential form it acquired in the William and Mary period – a slope-front desk surmounted by a cabinet having two doors and often a pediment. The double arched pediment, a stylistic feature of the period, is found on only a few pieces of American furniture. The shape of the mirrors at the top constitutes a thematic motif found also in the skirts of the high chests and dressing tables that we have already seen.

    Americans made and used many other types of furniture, such

62
63   as the **looking-glass with walnut veneer** at the Winterthur Museum and the **tall clock**, also at Winterthur, having brassworks by a clockmaker of Burlington, New Jersey. In a book of this scope, we can only sample from among those things that have survived, knowing that the most useful and many of the finest pieces have perished to time and disaster. Comments by contemporaries help to fill in and colour a picture that will always

have many gaps. What emerges from the evidence, at a date even earlier than our period, is a society of moderate but felt contrasts, variously selecting its models of thought and behaviour from Europe, particularly England, and producing furniture and other domestic articles of a quality that generally surpasses the productions of all other colonised regions of the Western Hemisphere, possibly because American colonials never allowed themselves to submit to a colonial mentality.

Tall clock. Brassworks by Isaac Pearson (about 1685–1749), Burlington, New Jersey. Case, walnut and pine, possibly New Jersey, height 80$\frac{5}{8}$ in. Later inscription inside the case gives a manufacture date of 1723. The Henry Francis du Pont Winterthur Museum, Delaware.

## Acknowledgements

The publishers would like to thank the following for granting permission to reproduce subjects illustrated in this book and for kindly supplying photographs: Albany Institute of History and Art, Albany, New York 38; Art Institute of Chicago 54; Baltimore Museum of Art, Baltimore, Maryland 44; Brooklyn Institute, New York 32–3; Colonial Williamsburg, Williamsburg, Virginia 11, 59 top and bottom; Essex Institute, Salem, Massachusetts 18; Craig Gilborn 8, 10; Henry Ford Museum, Dearborn, Michigan 48; Henry Francis du Pont Winterthur Museum, Winterthur, Delaware 2, 6, 12–13, 21–3, 25 top and bottom, 27, 29, 30, 37, 39, 43, 47, 49–53, 55, 58 top and bottom, 61–3; Historical Society of Pennsylvania, Philadelphia 20; Richard Merrill, Melrose, Massachusetts 31; Metropolitan Museum of Art, New York 16, 17, 19, 26, 35 top, 36, 42, 57; Museum of Early Southern Decorative Arts, Winston-Salem, North Carolina (photograph Old Salem Inc.) 46, Philadelphia Museum of Art 35, 40 top and bottom, 60.

COUNTRY LIFE COLLECTORS' GUIDES

Series editor Hugh Newbury
Series designer Ian Muggeridge

Published for Country Life Books by
THE HAMLYN PUBLISHING GROUP LIMITED
LONDON · NEW YORK · SYDNEY · TORONTO
Hamlyn House, Feltham, Middlesex, England

AMERICAN FURNITURE 1660–1725
ISBN 600434826
First published 1970
All rights reserved
Printed in Great Britain by Butler & Tanner Limited, Frome and London